ALL THINGS NICE

with Jo Seagar

NEW ZEALAND'S BAKING EXPERTS'
BEST EVER RECIPE COLLECTION

RANDOM HOUSE NEW ZEALAND LTD

Grateful acknowledgement is made to the
following suppliers of photographic props:
Country Road
Freedom Furniture
Living & Giving
Milly's Kitchen Shop
Stevens
The Garden Party
The Store

Special thanks for permission to use and adapt their recipes to
Alison Holst, Allyson Gofton, Chelsea Sugar, the Country Women's Institutes,
Dorothy Cashmore, the Edmonds Cookery Book, Jo Seagar,
Maureen Simpson.

New Zealand Sugar Company Limited
PO Box 30, Auckland 1015, New Zealand
Email chelsea@nzsugar.co.nz
www.chelsea.co.nz

The moral rights of the authors have been asserted.

A RANDOM HOUSE BOOK
published by
Random House New Zealand
18 Poland Road, Glenfield, Auckland, New Zealand
www.randomhouse.co.nz

First published 2002. Reprinted 2002, 2003, 2007, 2008
© 2002 New Zealand Sugar Company Limited

ISBN 978 1 86941 493 1

Introduction, tips and assistance with Best Ever recipe selection: Jo Seagar
Food Styling: Bernadette Hogg
Photography: Shaun Cato-Symonds
Design: Gianni Russo
Layout: Graeme Leather
Printed by Everbest in China

Contents

Introduction
5

Biscuits & Slices
7

Cakes
35

Muffins
53

Sweet Treats
63

Desserts
73

Jams, Pickles & Sauces
93

Index
110

INTRODUCTION

What an exciting project this has been, gathering together the Best Ever classic Kiwi recipes from New Zealand's baking experts into a book with glorious accompanying photographs. The best sponge cake, the best chocolate mousse: these are tried and true recipes that the panel thought were simply the best in their category and reflected great Kiwi baking traditions.

The tastes we remember with the most intense pleasure and nostalgia seem to be sweet old-fashioned baking favourites from childhood. Many recipes have a long colonial history going back over a hundred years, while others are comparative youngsters created by home cooks, cake shops and food writers in the last 20 or 30 years. They're all here – the pick of the bunch – along with loads of tips and hints to help you achieve the best results.

This is not a coffee-table book, nor one that will gather dust on a bookshelf. It is more likely to live close at hand in the kitchen, and a few splatters of cake mixture or a fine coating of icing sugar (Chelsea, of course!) will be the true measure of its wonderful resourceful value. I'm sure this will be a book you'll turn to again and again, and I trust you'll have as much fun trying the recipes as we had in gathering this collection together.

Happy baking.

Jo Seagar

BISCUITS & SLICES

A homemade biscuit or slice is almost always better than a bought one. They're so easy to make and they range from rich, gooey and scrumptious to crisp, oaty and healthy. Biscuits are probably one of the first things a child learns to cook, and a high success rate generates a great deal of satisfaction. There are some good old favourites here, plus a few new café-style recipes you'll be glad to have in your repertoire.

Afghans	8
Anzac Biscuits	9
Baby Pecan Pies	10
Caramel Slice	11
Chelsea Muesli Bars	12
Chocolate Chip Biscuits	13
Chocolate Chunk Oat Cookies	14
Chocolate Fudge Square	15
Chocolate Peppermint Slice	16
Coconut Macaroons	18
Double Chocolate Fudge Brownies	19
Ginger Crunch	20
Ginger Snaps	22
Hokey Pokey Biscuits	23
Louise Cake	24
Melting Moments	25
Meringues	26
Peanut Brownie Biscuits	28
Pikelets	29
Shortbread	30
Sugar-crusted Vanilla Cupcakes	31
Vanilla Custard Squares	32

Left: Coconut Macaroons

Afghans

MAKES 25–30 BISCUITS

100 g butter, softened
¼ cup Chelsea Caster Sugar
1 teaspoon vanilla essence
½ cup self-raising flour
¼ cup plain flour
1 teaspoon cocoa
1½ cups cornflakes, lightly crushed
1 tablespoon desiccated coconut
25–30 walnut halves

Preheat the oven to 180°C. In a large bowl, cream the butter, sugar and vanilla until light and fluffy. Sift in the flours and cocoa and stir in the cornflakes and coconut. Place heaped teaspoonfuls onto a well-greased baking tray. Squeeze the mixture together lightly if necessary — it may feel a little crumbly at this stage but it holds together when baked. Bake for 15–20 minutes. Cool on a wire rack and when cold spread with chocolate icing (see page 11) and top each one with a walnut half.

Jo's tip

DON'T STORE CRISP BISCUITS WITH SOFT ONES — THE CRISP ONES WILL SOFTEN.

Anzac Biscuits

Makes 40 biscuits

1 cup flour
1 cup Chelsea White Sugar
1¾ cups desiccated coconut (the coarsely shredded type is great for texture)
1½ cups rolled oats
¼ cup chopped walnuts
100 g butter
2 tablespoons Chelsea Golden Syrup
1 teaspoon baking soda
2 tablespoons boiling water

Preheat the oven to 160°C. Mix the flour, sugar, coconut, rolled oats and walnuts in a bowl. Melt the butter and golden syrup together. Stir the baking soda into the boiling water, then mix the butter and baking soda mixtures together in a large bowl. Add the flour mixture and combine. Roll teaspoonfuls of the mixture into small balls and place on a well-greased or baking-paper-lined oven tray. Press flat with the back of a spoon, allowing room for them to spread. Bake for 25–30 minutes. Cool on a wire rack and store in an airtight container.

A heritage recipe from New Zealand's cooking archives

Baby Pecan Pies

MAKES 16

125 g butter
1 cup flour
½ cup Chelsea Icing Sugar
1 cup pecans
60 g butter, melted
1 egg
1 cup Chelsea Soft Brown Sugar
1 teaspoon vanilla essence

Place the first measure of butter with the flour and icing sugar in a food processor and mix until the pastry forms a ball. Divide into 16 pieces and press each into the base and up the sides of a non-stick (or well-greased) mini muffin tin. Refrigerate for at least 30 minutes. Divide the pecans between the chilled pastry cases, breaking the nuts as required. Mix the melted butter, egg, brown sugar and vanilla until smooth and 'gluey' and spoon or pour carefully over the nuts. Do not overfill. Bake at 180°C for 20–25 minutes. Lift the pies from the tin and cool on a wire rack.

Jo's tip

STORING A SLICE OF RAW APPLE IN WITH THE BROWN SUGAR WILL STOP IT FROM HARDENING.

Caramel Slice

MAKES 30 PIECES

Base
125 g butter, softened
¼ cup Chelsea White Sugar
1 egg
1 cup flour
1 teaspoon baking powder
1 tablespoon cocoa

Filling
400 g (1 can) sweetened condensed milk
2 tablespoons Chelsea Golden Syrup
25 g butter
½ teaspoon vanilla essence

Preheat the oven to 180°C. First make the base. Cream the butter and sugar, add the egg and then the dry ingredients. Mix or process well. Press the mixture into the base of a well-greased and baking-paper-lined 20 x 30 cm sponge roll tin. Bake for 15 minutes.

While the base is cooking, prepare the caramel filling. Place all ingredients in a small saucepan and cook over a medium heat, stirring constantly, for 4–5 minutes until the mixture has thickened and become caramel-like. Pour this over the cooked base and return it to the oven to bake for a further 5 minutes. Remove from the oven and cool completely. When cold, ice with chocolate icing and cut into squares.

Chocolate Icing
2 cups Chelsea Icing Sugar
3 tablespoons cocoa
25 g butter, melted
boiling water

Mix the first 3 ingredients, adding enough boiling water to make a smooth paste.

A heritage recipe from New Zealand's cooking archives

Chelsea Muesli Bars

Makes 24 bars

125 g butter
1 cup Chelsea White Sugar
2 tablespoons Chelsea Golden Syrup
1 cup flour
1 teaspoon baking powder
1 cup desiccated coconut
1 egg
1 cup mixed dried fruit: raisins, currants, etc
$1\frac{1}{4}$ cups toasted muesli

Preheat the oven to 180°C. Put the butter, sugar and golden syrup in a large bowl and melt in the microwave. Thoroughly mix in the remaining ingredients. Grease a flat 20 x 30 cm sponge roll baking tin. Press the mixture into the tin and bake for 20 minutes. Cut into bars while still warm. Cool and store in an airtight container.

Jo's tip

TO PREVENT THE JAGGED EDGES YOU CAN GET WHEN CUTTING COOLED SLICES SUCH AS MUESLI SLICE, USE A SHARP KNIFE TIP TO SCORE THE BARS AS SOON AS THE TRAY COMES OUT OF THE OVEN. THEN CUT THE COOLED BARS ALONG THE SCORED LINES.

A Chelsea Sugar recipe

Chocolate Chip Biscuits

> **Jo's tip**
> PLACING A SLICE OF SOFT BREAD IN A PACKAGE OF HARDENED BROWN SUGAR WILL SOFTEN IT IN A COUPLE OF HOURS.

MAKES 30 BISCUITS

75 g butter, melted
½ cup Chelsea White Sugar
½ cup Chelsea Soft Brown Sugar
1 large egg
1 cup flour
½ teaspoon baking soda
½ cup chocolate chips

Preheat the oven to 180°C. Beat together the melted butter, sugars and egg. Sift the flour and baking soda and add with the chocolate chips to the butter mixture. Stir until well combined. Place teaspoonfuls on oven trays that have been lightly greased, sprayed or lined with baking paper. Leave room for the biscuits to spread. Bake for 8–10 minutes or until golden brown. Transfer to a wire rack. When cold, store in an airtight container.

Chocolate Chunk Oat Cookies

MAKES 24 LARGE COOKIES

250 g butter, softened
3 tablespoons sweetened condensed milk
¾ cup Chelsea White Sugar
1½ cups flour
1½ cups rolled oats
1 teaspoon baking powder
200 g dark chocolate, roughly chopped, or large chocolate chips

Preheat the oven to 180°C. Beat the butter, condensed milk and sugar together until light and creamy. Add the other ingredients and mix well. Place spoonfuls on a well-greased oven tray and flatten them. Cook for 15–20 minutes until golden brown. Cool on a wire rack and store in an airtight container.

Jo's tip

THE TUBES OF SWEETENED CONDENSED MILK ARE HANDY FOR RECIPES SUCH AS THIS THAT CALL FOR A SMALL QUANTITY.

Chocolate Fudge Square

MAKES 12–24 PIECES

½ cup Chelsea Soft Brown Sugar
¼ cup cocoa
3 tablespoons milk
75 g butter
1 packet malt, wine or plain digestive biscuits, crushed
1 cup chopped walnuts or sultanas, or a mixture
1 teaspoon vanilla essence

Mix the brown sugar and cocoa in a medium-sized saucepan, then add the milk and butter. Bring to the boil, stirring all the time. Remove from the heat, add the crushed biscuits, chopped nuts and/or sultanas and the vanilla. Mix well. Line a 20 x 30 cm sponge roll tin with baking paper. Press the mixture into the tin and flatten the surface with the back of a spoon. When cool, ice with chocolate icing (see page 11). Cut into squares when firm. Store in the refrigerator.

Chocolate Peppermint Slice

MAKES 24–36 PIECES

125 g dark chocolate
1 cup Chelsea White Sugar
150 ml can evaporated milk
2 teaspoons 100% pure corn syrup or liquid glucose
25 g butter
250 g dark chocolate, roughly chopped
100 g marshmallows (approx 1/2 packet), roughly chopped
oil of peppermint or peppermint essence (see note)

It is important that all ingredients are ready before you start to cook. Grease a 20 x 30 cm sponge roll or slice tin that has been lined with aluminium foil. This will make it easy to remove the slice from the tin.

Place the first measure of chocolate in a bowl over hot water to melt. Meanwhile, combine the sugar, evaporated milk, corn syrup or glucose and butter in a medium-sized saucepan. Stir over a medium heat without boiling until the sugar is dissolved. When the sugar has dissolved, increase the heat and bring the mixture to the boil, stirring constantly. Boil for *exactly 4 minutes*, stirring the mixture briskly the whole time. Remove the saucepan from the heat, quickly add the chopped chocolate and marshmallows and stir briskly until they have melted (this will only take a few minutes). Add the oil of peppermint or essence and mix well. Spread the mixture evenly in the tin with a spatula. Spread the melted chocolate evenly over the top. Refrigerate for 2 hours before cutting into small squares or sticks.

Jo's tip

OIL OF PEPPERMINT GIVES THE BEST TASTE. IT IS AVAILABLE FROM CHEMISTS OR HEALTH FOOD SHOPS. USE 4–6 DROPS FOR THIS RECIPE. PEPPERMINT ESSENCE IS AVAILABLE FROM SUPERMARKETS. START WITH ABOUT 4 DROPS, THEN TASTE BEFORE ADDING ANY MORE.

Coconut Macaroons

MAKES 30–40 BISCUITS

3 egg whites, at room temperature
¼ teaspoon salt
1 cup Chelsea Caster Sugar
½ teaspoon vanilla or almond essence
2 tablespoons flour
1½ cups desiccated coconut
40 blanched almonds

Preheat the oven to 150°C. Beat the egg whites with the salt until they form peaks that turn over, then add half the sugar and beat until the peaks stand upright when the beater is removed from the mixture. Stir in the essence. Mix together the remaining sugar, the flour and coconut, then fold this into the egg whites. Shape the mixture to form 30–40 biscuits and place on a well-greased baking tray. Try to keep them evenly round, and allow space for spreading. Top each biscuit with a blanched almond. Bake for 20–25 minutes. The biscuits should feel quite firm on the outside but be chewy inside. The larger the biscuits, the longer they will take to cook. Cool on a wire rack and store in an airtight container.

Jo's tip

NEVER USE A PLASTIC BOWL WHEN WHIPPING EGG WHITES: YOU WON'T GET THE VOLUME YOU REQUIRE.

Double Chocolate Fudge Brownies

MAKES 25–30 PIECES

250 g dark chocolate melts or chips
2 cups Chelsea Caster Sugar
4 eggs
1 teaspoon vanilla essence
¾ cup flour
¼ cup self-raising flour
½ cup cocoa
extra 125 g dark chocolate melts chopped
  or chocolate chips (the rest of the bag)
Chelsea Icing Sugar to decorate

> **Jo's tip**
> BROWNIE OR BISCUIT CRUMBS MAKE A GREAT ICE-CREAM TOPPING.

Preheat the oven to 160°C. Paper-line a 20 x 30 cm sponge roll tin. Melt the first measure of chocolate (I use the microwave). Beat the caster sugar, eggs and vanilla in a food processor or with a hand-held mixer. Add the melted chocolate, flours and cocoa. Stir in the extra chopped chocolate. Pour into the prepared tin and bake for 50 minutes until firm. Cool in the tin and cut into small bars or chunks. Store in an airtight container. Dust with icing sugar to serve.

Ginger Crunch

MAKES 24 PIECES

125 g butter, softened
½ cup Chelsea White Sugar
1½ cups Champion standard grade flour
1 teaspoon Edmonds baking powder
1 teaspoon ground ginger

GINGER ICING

75 g butter
1 cup Chelsea Icing Sugar
2 tablespoons Chelsea Golden Syrup
3 teaspoons ground ginger

Preheat the oven to 190°C. Cream the butter and sugar together until light and fluffy. Sift together the flour, baking powder and ginger. Mix into the creamed mixture. Turn the dough out onto a lightly floured board and knead well. Press into a greased 20 x 30 cm sponge roll tin. Bake for 20–25 minutes or until light brown. Pour ginger icing over while it is still hot and cut into squares before it gets cold.

Combine all ingredients in a small saucepan and heat until the butter has melted, stirring constantly.

Jo's tip

NO TIME TO WAIT FOR THE BUTTER TO SOFTEN? GRATE IT WITH A SMALL HAND-HELD GRATER INSTEAD.

Ginger Snaps

MAKES 45 BISCUITS

150 g butter
5 tablespoons Chelsea Golden Syrup
3½ cups flour
1 teaspoon baking soda
1 tablespoon ground ginger
2 cups Chelsea White Sugar
1 egg, beaten

Preheat the oven to 180°C. Heat the butter and golden syrup in a saucepan until almost boiling. Remove from heat. Sift the flour, baking soda and ginger into a large mixing bowl and stir in the sugar. Make a well in the centre and pour in the beaten egg, then the melted butter and syrup. Put aside to cool. Mix well. Roll the cooled biscuit mix into walnut-sized balls. Press them flat and place on cold, lightly greased oven trays. Allow room for them to spread. Bake for 15–20 minutes until they are a deep golden brown.

Jo's tip

RATHER THAN ROLLING OUT BISCUITS ON A FLOURED SURFACE, USE ICING SUGAR INSTEAD. YOU WILL END UP WITH A MORE TENDER BISCUIT.

A Chelsea Sugar recipe

Hokey Pokey Biscuits

MAKES 20–24 BISCUITS

125 g butter
1 cup Chelsea White Sugar
1 tablespoon Chelsea Golden Syrup
1 tablespoon milk
1½ cups Champion standard grade flour
1 teaspoon Edmonds baking soda

Preheat the oven to 180°C. Combine the butter, sugar, golden syrup and milk in a saucepan. Heat until butter is melted and the mixture is nearly boiling, stirring constantly. Remove from the heat and allow to cool to lukewarm. Sift the flour and baking soda together. Add to the cooled mixture. Stir well. Roll tablespoonfuls of mixture into balls and place on an ungreased baking tray. Press down lightly with a fork. Bake for 15–20 minutes or until golden brown.

Jo's tip

A RECIPE THAT INCLUDES BAKING SODA SHOULD BE PUT INTO THE OVEN AS SOON AS POSSIBLE AFTER MIXING AS THE LEAVENING ACTION STARTS TO TAKE EFFECT IMMEDIATELY UPON CONTACT WITH LIQUID.

Louise Cake

Makes 24 pieces

100 g butter
¼ cup Chelsea Caster Sugar
3 eggs, separated
1 teaspoon vanilla essence
2 cups self-raising flour
2 tablespoons milk
½ cup raspberry jam
¾ cup Chelsea Caster Sugar
¾ cup desiccated coconut

Preheat the oven to 180°C. Place the butter, the first measure of caster sugar, egg yolks and vanilla in a food processor and process until well mixed. Add the flour and milk and process to combine. Spread the mixture into a well-greased and baking-paper-lined 20 x 30 cm slice tin. Spread with the raspberry jam.

In a clean (non-plastic) bowl beat the egg whites until soft peaks form. Slowly add the second measure of caster sugar while continuing to beat until thick. Fold in the coconut. Spread this over the slice and bake for 25–30 minutes. Cool and slice into squares. Store in an airtight container.

Jo's tip

USE A FLAT METAL PASTRY SCRAPER TO CUT SQUARES AND BARS IN THEIR TINS. IT'S EASIER AND CLEANER THAN CUTTING THEM WITH A KNIFE AND IT CUTS RIGHT THROUGH TO THE BOTTOM.

Melting Moments

MAKES 24 BISCUITS

275 g butter, softened
½ cup Chelsea Icing Sugar
¼ teaspoon vanilla essence
1½ cups flour
½ cup cornflour

Preheat the oven to 160°C. Put the butter, icing sugar and vanilla into a food processor and process until creamy. Sift together the flour and cornflour and pulse into the creamed mixture. Do not over-process. Roll teaspoonfuls into balls and place on a greased baking tray. Press down lightly with a fork. Bake for 18–20 minutes until the biscuits are firm and lightly golden, but not brown. Cool on a wire rack and store in an airtight container.

Jo's tip

FOR AN EXTRA TREAT, SANDWICH TWO BISCUITS TOGETHER WITH ICING IN BETWEEN, SUCH AS GINGER ICING (PAGE 20), LEMON ICING (PAGE 47), VANILLA ICING (PAGE 32) OR CHOCOLATE ICING (PAGE 11).

Meringues

MAKES 36–40 MERINGUES

6 egg whites, at room temperature
2 cups Chelsea Caster Sugar
1 teaspoon vanilla essence
1 teaspoon vinegar
2 teaspoons cornflour
whipped cream to serve

Preheat the oven to 120°C. In a large metal, porcelain or glass (not plastic) bowl, beat the egg whites until soft peaks form. Gradually, a teaspoonful at a time, add the caster sugar. The mixture should be getting glossy, thick and shiny with each addition and the whole sugar-adding process should take at least 10 minutes. Beat in the vanilla, vinegar and cornflour. Spoon the mixture out in little blobs onto a baking-paper-covered tray. Bake for about 45 minutes until dry and crisp. The meringues should lift off the paper easily. Cool on a wire rack and stick them together in pairs with whipped cream when cold.

Jo's tip

WHEN STIFFLY BEATEN, EGG WHITES WILL EXPAND TO SIX TIMES THEIR UNWHIPPED VOLUME. BUT THEY WILL NOT WHIP UP IF EVEN A SPECK OF YOLK IS INCLUDED OR IF THE BOWL OR UTENSILS HAVE ANY OIL OR FAT ON THEM.

Peanut Brownie Biscuits

MAKES 20–25 BISCUITS

125 g butter, softened
1 cup Chelsea White Sugar
1 egg
1½ cups Champion standard grade flour
1 teaspoon Edmonds baking powder
pinch of salt
2 tablespoons cocoa
1 cup peanuts, roasted and shelled

Preheat the oven to 180°C. Cream the butter and sugar together until light and fluffy. Add the egg and beat well. Sift together the flour, baking powder, salt and cocoa and mix into the creamed mixture. Add the peanuts and mix well. Roll tablespoonfuls of the mixture into balls and place on greased oven trays. Flatten with a floured fork. Bake for 15 minutes or until cooked. Leave them to stand for about 5 minutes, then lift onto a wire rack. When cold, store in an airtight container.

Pikelets

MAKES 24 PIKELETS

1 teaspoon baking soda
1 cup milk
1 egg
3 tablespoons Chelsea White Sugar
2 cups flour
2 teaspoons cream of tartar

Dissolve the baking soda in the milk. Beat in the egg and sugar, then mix in the flour and cream of tartar. Mix to a smooth batter, using a little extra milk if required. Allow to rest for 10 minutes, then spoon onto a heated non-stick or well-greased heavy frying pan or crêpe pan. Cook over a medium heat until bubbles appear and the surface is golden brown. Turn and cook other side. Cool on a wire rack while you cook the rest of the batch.

Jo's tip

TEST BAKING SODA FOR FRESHNESS BY POURING ½ TEASPOON OF VINEGAR OR LEMON JUICE OVER SOME OF THE SODA. IF IT DOESN'T ACTIVELY BUBBLE, IT'S TIME TO BUY SOME MORE.

Shortbread

MAKES 20–24 PIECES

250 g butter, softened
¾ cup Chelsea Icing Sugar
½ cup cornflour
1½ cups flour

Preheat the oven to 150°C. Beat the butter and icing sugar together until creamy. Mix in the cornflour and flour. On a floured surface, roll the dough out to 1 cm thick and cut it into fingers. Carefully place these on a greased oven tray and prick them with a fork. Bake for 25–30 minutes, until pale but crisp. Cool on a wire rack and store in an airtight container.

Jo's tip

ALLOW BISCUITS TO COOL SLIGHTLY BEFORE REMOVING THEM FROM THE BAKING TRAY. AS SOON AS THEY ARE FIRM ENOUGH TO MOVE WITHOUT BREAKING, TRANSFER THEM TO A WIRE RACK TO COOL COMPLETELY. IF YOU LEAVE BISCUITS ON THE HOT BAKING TRAY THEY WILL CONTINUE TO COOK!

Sugar-crusted Vanilla Cupcakes

MAKES 12 CUPCAKES

a little sugar
4 eggs
1 cup Chelsea White Sugar
1 cup flour
½ teaspoon baking powder
1 teaspoon vanilla essence
extra sugar to sprinkle

Preheat the oven to 180°C. Well grease or oil spray 12 paper cupcases and sprinkle the sides and base of each with sugar. Beat the eggs with an electric beater until pale and fluffy. Slowly, one tablespoonful at a time, add the sugar and continue beating. Fold in the flour and baking powder, then stir in the vanilla. Pour into the cupcases (these stand up beautifully if placed in a muffin tin). Sprinkle the extra sugar lightly over the surface and bake for 20–25 minutes. The top should be crackled, golden and crusty. Cool on a wire rack.

A Chelsea Sugar recipe

Vanilla Custard Squares

MAKES 16 SQUARES

3 sheets frozen pre-rolled flaky puff pastry, thawed
1 cup custard powder
5 cups milk
1 cup Chelsea White Sugar
2 teaspoons vanilla essence

Preheat the oven to 200°C. For best results use a 23–25 cm square tin with a removable base. Otherwise, trim the pastry to 2–3 cm larger than your cake tin.

First we need to pre-cook the pastry. Place the sheets on greased oven trays and prick all over with a fork. Place a fine wire-mesh cooling rack over each sheet so it rises and puffs up evenly. (This step is not essential but it does produce a very professional finish.) Bake the pastry for 8–10 minutes or until puffed and golden. Trim the edges with a sharp knife so they fit snugly in your cake tin. Place one sheet in the base of the tin.

To make the filling, mix the custard powder to a smooth paste with a little of the milk. Separately heat the rest of the milk and add the sugar to it. With a wire whisk, stir the custard powder paste into the warmed milk and continue to heat and stir until boiling and thickened. Remove from the heat and add the vanilla. Pour half the custard over the pastry base, then lay on the second pastry sheet. Pour over the remaining custard and place the third pastry sheet on the top. Press down gently to settle the layers and leave to cool. Then refrigerate until quite cold and set. Ice with vanilla icing when very chilled.

Vanilla Icing

2 cups Chelsea Icing Sugar
25 g butter, softened
¼ teaspoon vanilla essence
boiling water to mix

Mix the icing sugar, butter and vanilla in a bowl, then stir in small amounts of the water until you get the right consistency. Ice the top layer of pastry when the custard filling has been chilled completely. Leave for one hour, then carefully remove from the tin using a sharp knife to ease away from the edges. Cut into squares. Refrigerate squares until served.

CAKES

A cake is a symbol of celebration. It can be lit with candles to mark another birthday, bedecked with cherubs to bless a marriage, frosted in soft pastel icing to welcome a baby, or decorated with snowy scenes and jolly Santas to celebrate the Christmas season. Cakes have been a part of our cooking history since early New Zealand settlement times. The ones in this book are the favourites of our panel of testers and tasters: classic recipes no such book should be without. We've included two chocolate cakes, one for big celebrations and a classic chocolate cake that's so quick and easy to throw together. So, it's out with the beaters, bowls and wooden spoons to whisk up a fabulous nostalgic treat for your family and loved ones.

Apple Cinnamon Cake	36
Carrot Cake	37
Celebration Chocolate Cake	38
Classic Chocolate Cake	39
Date & Walnut Loaf	40
Gingerbread	42
Lemon Syrup Loaf	43
Marble Cake	45
Mississippi Mud Cake	46
Moist Banana Cake	47
Rich Christmas Cake	48
Sponge Cake	50
Sultana Cake	51

Left: Carrot Cake

Apple Cinnamon Cake

150 g butter, melted
2 cups well-drained slightly stewed apple
  or canned apple-pie filling
1 cup Chelsea White Sugar
2 eggs
2 cups flour
2 teaspoons ground cinnamon
2 teaspoons baking powder
½ cup sultanas
½ cup walnuts
Chelsea Icing Sugar to dust

Preheat the oven to 160°C. Mix all the ingredients together and spoon into a well-greased or baking-paper-lined 20–23 cm cake tin. Bake for 55–60 minutes until golden and a skewer inserted into the centre of the cake comes out clean. Cool on a wire rack. Serve warm, dusted with icing sugar.

Jo's tip

SPRINKLE CUT APPLES OR BANANAS WITH LEMON JUICE TO PREVENT THEM TURNING BROWN BEFORE YOU USE THEM.

Carrot Cake

¾ cup self-raising flour
¾ cup wholemeal flour
1 teaspoon mixed spice
½ teaspoon ground cinnamon
½ teaspoon ground ginger
1 teaspoon baking soda
1 cup Chelsea Caster Sugar
3 large eggs
1 cup sunflower or canola oil
1 teaspoon vanilla essence
¾ cup chopped walnuts
2 cups grated carrot
½ cup sultanas or raisins
2 tablespoons desiccated coconut

Preheat the oven to 180°C. Sift the flours, spices and baking soda into a large mixing bowl. Add all the remaining ingredients and stir with a wooden spoon until just combined — don't beat. Line a 20–23 cm cake tin (6 cm deep) with baking paper and grease well. Pour the mixture into the prepared tin and smooth the surface. Bake for 1 hour or until a skewer inserted into the centre of the cake comes out clean. Remove from the oven and cool. Spread the top with cream cheese frosting.

CREAM CHEESE FROSTING

125 g cream cheese, softened
50 g butter, softened
2½ cups Chelsea Icing Sugar

Beat all ingredients together until smooth.

Celebration Chocolate Cake

MAKES 2 LARGE CAKES: IDEAL FOR GROUPS OR PARTIES.

2 cups Chelsea Caster Sugar
3 cups self-raising flour
2 teaspoons baking soda
½ cup cocoa
3 eggs, separated
2 cups milk
2 tablespoons vinegar
2 tablespoons Chelsea Golden Syrup
2 teaspoons vanilla
1½ cups cooking oil (canola is ideal)
1 egg
whipped cream and icing of your choice

Preheat the oven to 180°C. Combine all the dry ingredients. In a large bowl beat the 3 egg whites until stiff. In a separate bowl, combine the milk and vinegar, then add the rest of the wet ingredients, including the 3 egg yolks and whole egg, and beat. Mix the wet and dry ingredients together, then fold in the beaten egg whites. Pour equal amounts of mixture into two well-greased or baking-paper-lined 20–23cm cake tins. Bake for 25–30 minutes. Cool on a wire rack. To serve, pile some whipped cream on one cake, place the other cake on top and ice (see Chocolate Icing, page 11).

Jo's tip

SPREAD WARM STRAWBERRY JAM OVER THE TOP OF THE BASE CAKE FOR AN EVEN MORE DELICIOUS FLAVOUR.

Classic Chocolate Cake

120 g butter, softened
½ cup Chelsea White Sugar
1 egg
2 tablespoons Chelsea Golden Syrup
2 cups flour
2 tablespoons cocoa
1 teaspoon baking soda
1 cup milk
1 teaspoon baking powder

Preheat the oven to 180°C. Beat the butter and sugar together. Add the egg and golden syrup and mix well. Sift in the flour and cocoa. Dissolve the baking soda in the milk and add to the mixture. Beat together until smooth. Add the baking powder. Bake in a well-greased and baking-paper-lined 20–23 cm cake tin for 40–45 minutes. Cool and ice with chocolate icing (see page 11) when cold.

Jo's tip

IF YOU'RE HAVING A PROBLEM WITH ICING STICKING TO YOUR SPREADER, DIP IT BRIEFLY IN HOT WATER. THE ICING WILL SLIDE RIGHT OFF.

Date & Walnut Loaf

75 g butter
1 cup chopped, pitted dates
¾ cup Chelsea Soft Brown Sugar
finely grated rind of 1 orange
1 cup boiling water
1 egg
2 cups flour
3 teaspoons baking powder
½ teaspoon salt
½ cup chopped walnuts

Preheat the oven to 180°C. Cut the butter into cubes and put it in a bowl with the dates, brown sugar and orange rind. Pour over the boiling water and leave to stand for about 10 minutes, stirring occasionally, until the butter melts. Cool to room temperature.

Meanwhile, line the long sides and bottom of a 7-cup (1.75-litre) loaf tin with a strip of baking paper. Butter or spray the ends of the tin.

Beat the egg until frothy. Mix the remaining ingredients together, then add them with the egg to the cooled date mixture. Fold the three mixtures together lightly, stirring until everything is just dampened but not smooth (if it is overmixed the loaf will rise to a peak and be tough).

Turn into the prepared tin and bake for about 40 minutes, or until a skewer inserted into the centre of the loaf comes out clean.

Jo's tip

A SUBSTITUTE FOR 1 TEASPOON BAKING POWDER: ½ TEASPOON CREAM OF TARTAR PLUS ¼ TEASPOON BAKING SODA.

Gingerbread

125 g butter
½ cup Chelsea White Sugar
1 cup Chelsea Treacle
½ cup milk
3 cups flour
1¼ teaspoons baking soda
1 tablespoon ground ginger
¼ teaspoon ground cinnamon
¼ teaspoon ground cloves
Chelsea Icing Sugar to dust

Preheat the oven to 160°C. Line a 23 cm square cake tin or small roasting dish with non-stick baking paper. Heat the butter, sugar and treacle together in a saucepan until the butter is just melted. Remove the pan from heat and stir in the milk. Cool slightly. Sift the dry ingredients into a bowl. Make a well in the centre and tip in the liquid ingredients. Mix quickly and don't overmix. Pile the mixture into the prepared tin and bake for 45–50 minutes until the gingerbread is nicely risen and a skewer inserted into the centre comes out clean. Cool in the tin for 10–15 minutes before tipping out onto a cake rack. Dust with icing sugar to serve.

A Chelsea Sugar recipe

Lemon Syrup Loaf

1 cup Chelsea Caster Sugar
grated rind of 2 lemons
100 g butter, softened
2 eggs
½ cup milk
1¾ cups self-raising flour
¼ teaspoon salt
¼ cup lemon juice
¼ cup Chelsea Caster Sugar

Preheat the oven to 180°C. In a food processor mix the first measure of caster sugar and the lemon rind. Add the butter and process until creamy. Add the eggs, milk, flour and salt.

Line a 21 x 12 cm loaf tin with baking paper (run the paper down one end, along the bottom and out the other end, leaving overhangs; repeat for the sides). Grease the paper and pour in the mixture. Bake for 50–60 minutes or until cooked when the loaf shrinks from the sides of the tin.

While the loaf bakes, mix the lemon juice with the ¼ cup caster sugar. As soon as you remove the loaf from the oven drizzle this mixture over its surface. Remove the loaf from the tin by lifting the paper and cool on a wire rack. Serve with fresh lemon curd (see page 95).

A Chelsea Sugar recipe

Marble Cake

3 eggs
¾ cup Chelsea White Sugar
1 cup Champion standard grade flour
1 teaspoon Edmonds baking powder
50 g butter, melted
2 tablespoons boiling water
1 tablespoon cocoa
2–3 drops red food colouring

Preheat the oven to 190°C. Beat the eggs until thick. Gradually beat in sugar until the mixture is very thick and white. Sift in the flour and baking powder and combine. Fold in the butter and boiling water. Divide the mixture into three equal amounts. Into one third stir the cocoa; to another third add enough red food colouring to make a pink mixture. Leave the last third plain. Spoon the three mixtures in diagonal strips into a greased and lined 20 cm square cake tin. Using a knife, twirl together the three mixtures. Bake for 20–25 minutes or until the cake springs back when lightly touched. Leave in the tin for 10 minutes before turning out onto a wire rack. When cool, ice with chocolate icing (see page 11).

Jo's tip

TO HELP CAKES COME OUT FLAT ON TOP FOR DECORATING, LIGHTLY DROP THE FILLED TIN ON THE BENCH THREE OR FOUR TIMES BEFORE PLACING IN THE OVEN. THIS HELPS REMOVE EXTRA AIR BUBBLES IN THE MIXTURE.

Mississippi Mud Cake

2 teaspoons instant coffee powder
1¼ cups hot water
¼ cup whisky or fruit juice
175 g cooking chocolate
250 g unsalted butter
2 cups Chelsea White Sugar
2 cups flour
1 teaspoon baking soda
2 eggs
1 teaspoon vanilla essence
Chelsea Icing Sugar to dust

Preheat the oven to 140°C. Put the coffee powder, hot water and whisky or fruit juice into a saucepan and bring to a simmer. Add the broken chocolate and butter and stir until melted. Add the sugar and stir until it has dissolved. Remove the mixture from the heat and allow to cool. Sift the flour and baking soda together into a large bowl and make a well in the centre. In a separate bowl, beat the eggs together with the vanilla and stir into the chocolate mixture. Pour the chocolate mixture into the well in the dry ingredients and stir to mix.

Pour the mixture into a well-greased and floured 23 cm cake tin. Bake for 1¼–1¾ hours until the cake has shrunk from the sides of the tin and is firm to the touch. Cool in the tin for 20 minutes before turning out onto a wire rack. Dust with icing sugar to serve.

Allyson Gofton

Moist Banana Cake

125 g butter, softened
1 cup Chelsea White Sugar
2 eggs
3 bananas, mashed (approx. 2 cups)
2 teaspoons baking soda
2 tablespoons hot milk
2 cups flour
1 teaspoon baking powder

Lemon Icing

2 tablespoons lemon juice
1 teaspoon butter
2 cups Chelsea Icing Sugar
1 teaspoon grated lemon rind

Preheat the oven to 180°C. Cream the butter and sugar until light and fluffy. Add the eggs one at a time, mixing well after each addition. Stir in the mashed banana and mix well. Stir the baking soda into the hot milk and add this to the mixture. Lastly, fold in the flour and baking powder.

Pour into a well-greased 20–21 cm tin with the base lined with baking paper. Bake for 45–50 minutes, until the cake springs back when lightly pressed. Cool for 15 minutes in the tin, then carefully turn the cake out and cool it completely on a wire rack. Ice with lemon icing when completely cool.

Heat the lemon juice and butter and stir until the butter has melted. Mix all the ingredients together to reach a smooth, spreadable consistency (add a few drops of water if it is too firm).

A heritage recipe from New Zealand's cooking archives

Rich Christmas Cake

1.5 kg mixed dried fruit
250 g glacé cherries, red and green
100 g mixed peel
1 tablespoon grated orange rind
1 tablespoon grated lemon rind
½ cup brandy or dark rum
500 g butter, softened
1½ cups Chelsea Soft Brown or Dark Cane Sugar
8 eggs
2 bananas, mashed
2 teaspoons vanilla essence
4 cups flour
1 cup self-raising flour
almonds to decorate (optional)

Place the dried fruit, cherries, mixed peel, orange rind, lemon rind and brandy in a large bowl and mix well. Cover and leave overnight.

Preheat the oven to 150°C. Cream the butter and sugar until light and fluffy, then add the eggs one at a time, beating well after each addition, then add the banana and vanilla. Stir the fruit mixture into this and mix well. Add the flours and mix until well combined. Place in a deep 25 cm cake tin that has been lined with baking paper. Wrap the base and sides of the tin in four or five sheets of newspaper tied around with string. If you wish, decorate with almonds. Bake for about 3½ hours, or until a skewer inserted into the middle of the cake comes out clean.

Jo's tip

WHEN CUTTING BAKING PAPER TO LINE ROUND CAKE TINS TRACE THE BOTTOM OF THE TIN ONTO BAKING PAPER. FOLD THE TRACED CIRCLE IN HALF AND IN HALF AGAIN, THEN CUT JUST OUTSIDE THE OUTLINE OF THE QUARTER CIRCLE.

Sponge Cake

4 large eggs, separated (room temperature)
¾ cup Chelsea White Sugar
¾ cup cornflour
2 tablespoons custard powder
3 teaspoons baking powder
whipped cream to serve
fresh fruit to serve
Chelsea Icing Sugar to dust

Preheat the oven to 180°C. Well grease two 23 cm sandwich cake tins and line them with baking paper. Beat the egg whites until stiff. Slowly add the sugar and beat until mixture is stiff and glossy. Add the yolks one at a time and mix each in well. In a separate bowl, sift together the cornflour, custard powder and baking powder. Gently fold the dry ingredients into the egg mixture, using a metal spoon. Pour half the mixture into each prepared tin and bake for 15–20 minutes without opening the oven door. When cooked the cakes should shrink slightly from the sides of the tins and spring back when touched gently.

Cool for 10 minutes in the tin, then turn out onto a wire rack covered with a tea-towel or paper towel to prevent a rack imprint on the sponges. When cool, fill with whipped cream and fruit and sprinkle with a fine dusting of icing sugar.

Sultana Cake

500 g sultanas
water to cover
250 g butter, softened
1¼ cups Chelsea Caster Sugar
2 teaspoons lemon juice
1 teaspoon grated lemon rind
1 teaspoon vanilla essence
3 eggs
2 cups flour
½ cup self-raising flour
¼ cup milk
¼ cup candied peel

Preheat the oven to 180°C. Place the sultanas in a bowl or saucepan and just cover with water. Bring to the boil and simmer for 5 minutes. Drain and cool.

Cream the butter and sugar until light and fluffy. Add the lemon juice, lemon rind and vanilla. Add the eggs one at a time, beating well after each addition. Stir in the flours and milk, then the sultanas and candied peel. Pour into a well-greased 21–23 cm square cake tin with the base lined with baking paper. Bake for 1 hour, then reduce the temperature to 160°C and bake for a further 50–60 minutes, or until a skewer inserted into the centre of the cake comes out clean. Cool in the tin and store in an airtight container.

Fruitcakes like this are best left for 12 hours before slicing.

A heritage recipe from New Zealand's cooking archives

MUFFINS

Perfect muffins are a happy balance between moistness and flavour. You can run up a batch in a jiffy and there is nothing nicer than the smell of muffins baking! In terms of flavouring it almost seems as if anything goes: if ingredients go well together then you can combine them in a muffin. They're best eaten fresh and warm, straight from the oven. Here's a selection of some of the best muffins in town.

Apricot Crunch Muffins	54
Banana Bran Muffins	55
Blueberry Muffins	56
Chocolate Chip Muffins	57
Crunchy Lemon Poppyseed Muffins	58
Jaffa Muffins	60
White Chocolate Chunk Muffins	61

Left: White Chocolate Chunk Muffins

Apricot Crunch Muffins

MAKES 12 MUFFINS

½ cup chopped dried apricots
½ cup water
½ cup apricot jam
100 g butter
1 egg
½ cup Chelsea White Sugar
½ cup milk
2 cups flour
4 teaspoons baking powder
2 tablespoons Chelsea Raw Sugar

Preheat the oven to 180°C. Place the apricots, water and jam in a large saucepan. Bring to the boil and simmer for 5 minutes. Stir in the butter and stir until it melts. Remove from the heat and mix in the egg, sugar and milk. Add the flour and baking powder and mix until just combined – don't overmix. Spoon into well-greased muffin tins. Sprinkle top with raw sugar and bake for 15–20 minutes. Cool on a wire rack.

A Chelsea Sugar recipe

Banana Bran Muffins

MAKES 12 MUFFINS

¾ cup Chelsea White Sugar
1 cup bran
1 cup flour
4 teaspoons baking powder
2 eggs
100 g butter, melted
½ cup milk
2 bananas, mashed

Preheat the oven to 200°C. Mix all the dry ingredients together in a bowl. In a separate bowl, beat the eggs, melted butter and milk together with the bananas. Add the dry ingredients and mix together to just combine. Spoon into well-greased muffin tins and bake for 10–15 minutes.

Jo's tip

FOR MUFFINS THAT SLIDE RIGHT OUT OF THEIR TINS, PLACE THE HOT MUFFIN TINS ON A WET TOWEL FOR A SECOND BEFORE TURNING OVER.

Blueberry Muffins

Makes 12 muffins

2 cups flour
4 teaspoons baking powder
1 cup Chelsea Caster Sugar
1 egg
¼ cup oil
1½ cups milk
1 teaspoon grated lemon rind
2 teaspoons lemon juice
1½ cups blueberries (see note)
Chelsea Icing Sugar to dust

Preheat the oven to 200°C. Mix all ingredients together in a large bowl until just combined and moistened. Don't overmix or the muffins will be tough and will rise unevenly. Spoon into well-greased muffin tins and bake for 15–18 minutes. Cool on a wire rack and dust with icing sugar to serve.

NOTE: Blueberries can be fresh, canned or frozen. If using frozen, use them straight from the freezer (no need to thaw). Canned blueberries need to be well drained.

Chocolate Chip Muffins

Makes 12 muffins

2 cups flour
4 teaspoons baking powder
pinch salt
100 g butter
¾ cup Chelsea Caster Sugar
2 eggs
½ teaspoon vanilla essence
½ cup chocolate chips
1 cup milk

Preheat the oven to 220°C. Mix all the ingredients together in a large bowl until just combined and moistened. Don't overmix or the muffins will be tough and will rise unevenly. Spoon into well-greased muffin tins and bake for 12–15 minutes until cooked. Serve warm.

Jo's tip

IF YOU WANT THE CHOCOLATE CHIPS IN BISCUITS AND MUFFINS TO RETAIN THEIR SHAPE BETTER, FREEZE THEM BEFORE ADDING TO THE MIXTURE.

Crunchy Lemon Poppyseed Muffins

MAKES 12 MUFFINS

2 cups self-raising flour
1 cup Chelsea White Sugar
½ cup poppyseeds
finely grated rind of 2 lemons
100 g butter, melted
1 cup milk
2 large eggs
juice of 2 lemons
¼ cup Chelsea White Sugar

Preheat the oven to 200°C. Mix the first four ingredients in a large bowl. In a second bowl mix the melted butter, milk and eggs. Tip the liquid ingredients into the dry ingredients and lightly fold together until flour is dampened. Do not overmix. Spoon into well-greased muffin tins and bake for 10–15 minutes.

While the muffins cook, mix the lemon juice and the second measure of sugar (do not dissolve the sugar). As soon as muffins have been removed from the tins, brush them with lemon sugar topping. Cool on a wire rack.

Jo's tip

AFTER SQUEEZING LEMONS FOR COOKING, FREEZE THE RINDS. WHENEVER YOU NEED FRESHLY GRATED LEMON RIND YOU CAN GRATE IT FROM THE FROZEN LEMONS AND SAVE YOURSELF HAVING TO USE UP A LEMON JUST FOR ITS RIND.

Jaffa Muffins

Makes 12 muffins

2½ cups flour
4 teaspoons baking powder
¾ cup Chelsea White Sugar
1 egg
¼ cup oil
¾ cup milk
½ cup freshly squeezed orange juice
finely grated rind of 2 oranges
½ cup chocolate chips

Preheat the oven to 200°C. Mix all the ingredients in a large bowl until just combined — don't overmix. Spoon into well-greased muffin tins and bake for 12–15 minutes. Cool on a wire rack.

Jo's tip

COOL BAKED GOODS COMPLETELY BEFORE FREEZING OR THEY WILL END UP SOGGY.

A Chelsea Sugar recipe

White Chocolate Chunk Muffins

Makes 12 muffins

¼ cup cocoa
2 cups flour
4 teaspoons baking powder
100 g butter, melted
¾ cup Chelsea White Sugar
2 eggs
½ teaspoon vanilla essence
1 cup milk
1 cup white chocolate chips or chopped white chocolate pieces

Preheat the oven to 200°C. Mix all ingredients together in a large bowl until just combined and moistened. Spoon into well-greased muffin tins and bake for 15–18 minutes. Cool on a wire rack.

Sweet Treats

The lure of homemade sweet treats is as irresistible today as ever. A sweet stall spells instant financial success for a fundraising event. Who can possibly resist creamy Russian fudge, delectable coconut ice or crunchy hokey pokey? So, whether it's a trip down memory lane for a nostalgic taste of childhood, fuel for a fundraising fête or a special treat or gift for someone you love, we've got all the best recipes covered here.

Apricot Balls	64
Chocolate Fudge	65
Chocolate Prune & Port Truffles	66
Chocolate Rum & Raisin Balls	68
Coconut Ice	69
Hokey Pokey	70
Russian Fudge	71

Left: Coconut Ice

Apricot Balls

MAKES 36 BALLS

250 g dried apricots, chopped into small pieces
¾ cup orange juice
½ teaspoon citric acid
1 cup Chelsea Icing Sugar
1 cup desiccated coconut
1 cup finely crushed biscuit crumbs
1 extra cup desiccated coconut for rolling

Place the apricots, orange juice and citric acid in a saucepan and bring to the boil. Reduce the heat and simmer for 15 minutes. Leave until cool, then place in a food processor or blender and purée. Transfer to a large bowl and add the icing sugar, coconut and biscuit crumbs. Mix well. Roll into walnut-size balls and coat well in the second measure of coconut. Store in the refrigerator.

A Chelsea Sugar recipe

Chocolate Fudge

MAKES 30 PIECES

2 cups Chelsea White Sugar
2 tablespoons cocoa
½ cup milk
25 g butter
½ teaspoon vanilla essence

Place the sugar and cocoa in a saucepan and mix to combine. Add the milk and butter. Heat gently, stirring constantly until the sugar has dissolved and butter melted. Bring to the boil. Let the mixture boil without stirring until it reaches the soft-ball stage (120°C). Remove from the heat. Add the vanilla and leave to stand for 5 minutes. Beat with a wooden spoon until thick and pour into a well-greased tin. Mark into squares. Cut when cold.

Jo's tip

USING A SUGAR THERMOMETER TAKES THE GUESSWORK OUT OF SWEET-MAKING AND ENSURES EXCELLENT RESULTS.

Chocolate Prune & Port Truffles

MAKES 40–50 TRUFFLES

375 g dark chocolate
200 g butter
20 pitted prunes (orange-flavoured ones are great)
¼ cup port (or orange juice)
3 cups Chelsea Icing Sugar
750 g dark chocolate, to dip truffles

Jo's tip

TAKE CARE WHEN MELTING CHOCOLATE OR YOU CAN EASILY END UP WITH A GRAINY MESS. THE LIGHTER THE CHOCOLATE, THE HIGHER THE CHANCES OF THIS HAPPENING. CHOCOLATE MELTS BETTER AND FASTER AT LOWER TEMPERATURES. NEVER LET YOUR CHOCOLATE GET ABOVE 40°C.

Place the chocolate and butter in a microwave-safe bowl and microwave until melted (about 4 minutes). Stir a couple of times during cooking. Chop up the prunes, checking there are no stones remaining, and place in a small microwave-safe bowl with the port. Microwave for 2–3 minutes to plump them up. Mix the prunes in with the chocolate and butter and add the icing sugar. Stir until well combined. Chill until firm enough to roll into walnut-sized balls (30–60 minutes). If the mixture goes too solid, microwave it on medium to soften it to the right consistency.

Place the balls of mixture on a foil-lined tray and freeze until really solid (about 2 hours). Melt the remaining chocolate in the microwave on medium–low power, stirring often (or melt over a bowl of hot water). Dip the frozen truffles in the melted chocolate. Drip off the excess chocolate and put them back on the foil-lined tray to harden. Do not store the finished truffles in the refrigerator as the chocolate tends to sweat. Keep in a cool place.

Chocolate Rum & Raisin Balls

Makes about 50 balls

200 g butter
200 g dark chocolate chips
¼ cup rum (or 2 teaspoons rum essence)
3 cups Chelsea Icing Sugar
1 cup raisins or sultanas, finely chopped
1 cup desiccated coconut for rolling

Melt the butter and chocolate chips together, either in the microwave or over a saucepan of gently simmering water. Add the rum, icing sugar and raisins, mixing well. Chill the mixture until you can shape it into small balls the size of a large marble. Roll them in coconut and store in the fridge.

A Chelsea Sugar recipe

Coconut Ice

MAKES 25–30 PIECES

100 g butter
1 cup milk
6 cups Chelsea Icing Sugar
1 teaspoon salt
1 cup desiccated coconut
2 teaspoons coconut essence

Place the butter, milk, icing sugar and salt in a medium-sized saucepan and heat gently until the sugar dissolves. Bring the mixture to the boil and keep the heat sufficient to just maintain the boil, stirring only occasionally, until the mixture reaches soft-ball stage (120°C). Add the coconut and coconut essence and remove from the heat. Cool for 5–10 minutes, then beat until the mixture thickens. Pour into a greased tin about 20 x 20 cm. Allow to cool and cut into squares.

NOTE: For pink coconut ice add a drop of red food colouring with the coconut. For the traditional two-tone effect make a batch of white and then a batch of pink, pouring the pink on top of the set white.

Hokey Pokey

MAKES 15–20 CHUNKS

5 tablespoons Chelsea White Sugar
2 tablespoons Chelsea Golden Syrup
1 teaspoon Edmonds baking soda

Put the sugar and golden syrup in a saucepan. Heat gently, stirring constantly until the sugar has dissolved. Increase the heat and bring to the boil. Boil for 2 minutes. Stir occasionally, if necessary, to prevent burning. Remove from the heat and add the baking soda. Stir quickly until the mixture froths up, which it will do rapidly! Pour immediately into a greased tin. Leave until cold and hard, then break into pieces.

Jo's tip

MEASURING HONEY OR GOLDEN SYRUP IS EASIER IF YOU FIRST SPRAY THE MEASURING CUP OR SPOON WITH OIL.

Russian Fudge

MAKES 36 PIECES

3½ cups Chelsea White Sugar
125 g butter
3 tablespoons Chelsea Golden Syrup
½ cup milk
½ teaspoon salt
200 g sweetened condensed milk
  (½ a standard can)
2 teaspoons vanilla essence

Place all the ingredients except the vanilla in a medium-heavy saucepan. Warm over a gentle heat until the sugar has dissolved. Bring to a gentle boil and cook for about 15–20 minutes until it reaches the soft-ball stage (120°C). Remove from the heat and add the vanilla. Beat (I use an electric mixer) until the fudge is creamy and thick and has lost its gloss. Pour into a greased 20 cm cake tin. Score the top and break into pieces when cold.

Jo's tip

USING A SUGAR THERMOMETER TAKES THE GUESSWORK OUT OF SWEET-MAKING AND ENSURES EXCELLENT RESULTS.

DESSERTS

Any meal occasion deserves to be rounded off well, and how better than with a delicious dessert? Covering everything from delicious old-fashioned sticky pudding favourites to smart café-style concoctions, the next few pages will open the floodgates on wistful food memories. For every chocoholic there is also a lemonophile, and we've got you well catered for too. There are lots of great desserts from the past as well as tempting new ideas to get those tastebuds tingling. So come on, eat up your meat and veges so you, too, can indulge . . .

Apple Crumble	74
Bread & Butter Pudding	75
Chocolate Mousse	76
Chocolate Self-saucing Pudding	77
Christmas Pudding	78
Citrus Tart	81
Crème Caramel	82
Golden Syrup Steamed Pudding	83
Lemon Cheesecake	84
Lemon Delicious Pudding	86
Lemon Meringue Pie	87
Pavlova	88
Rice Pudding	89
Sticky Date Pudding with Butterscotch Sauce	90

Left: Chocolate Mousse

Apple Crumble

SERVES 4

BASE
4 cups peeled, thinly sliced apple
¼ cup Chelsea Caster Sugar
½ teaspoon mixed spice
¼ cup water

CRUMBLE TOPPING
1 cup flour
½ cup Chelsea Dark Cane Sugar
1 cup desiccated coconut
75 g cold butter, cut into cubes

Preheat the oven to 180°C. Place the apple slices in a well-greased pie dish and sprinkle with the caster sugar, mixed spice and water. In a food processor, mix the topping ingredients until the mixture resembles coarse breadcrumbs. Sprinkle the crumble topping over the fruit and bake for 45–50 minutes until the topping is firm and light golden brown. Serve warm with whipped cream or ice-cream.

A heritage recipe from New Zealand's cooking archives

Bread & Butter Pudding

SERVES 4

6 slices white sandwich bread, buttered
2 tablespoons currants
2 tablespoons sultanas
2 eggs
2 tablespoons Chelsea White Sugar
2 cups milk
1 teaspoon vanilla essence
½ teaspoon grated nutmeg
Chelsea Icing Sugar to dust

Preheat the oven to 180°C. Cut the crusts off the bread and cut each slice in half diagonally to make 2 triangles. Lay four bread triangles butter side down in a pie dish or small lasagne dish, approximately 20 x 20 cm. Sprinkle with half the currants and sultanas and repeat to form layers. Finish with a layer of bread with the butter side up. Beat the eggs and sugar together, then add the milk and vanilla. Pour over the bread and butter and sprinkle the top with grated nutmeg. Place the dish into a large roasting pan filled with water to come three-quarters of the way up the sides of the pie dish. Bake for 30 minutes until golden brown and set. Dust with icing sugar to serve.

Chocolate Mousse

SERVES 4–6

200 g cooking chocolate
4 eggs, separated
300 ml cream
2 tablespoons Chelsea White Sugar

Break the chocolate into the top of a double-boiler. Stir over hot water in the bottom of the double-boiler until the chocolate has melted. Allow to cool slightly. Stir in the egg yolks and beat until thick and smooth. Whip the cream and quickly fold the chocolate mixture into it. In a separate bowl, beat the egg whites until stiff but not dry. Gradually add the sugar, beating until thick and glossy. Fold half the egg white mixture into the chocolate mixture, then add the rest, folding gently. Pour into four-to-six individual coffee cups or one large dish. Chill until firm.

Jo's tip

WHEN WHIPPING CREAM, PLACE THE BOWL ON A FOLDED, DAMPENED TOWEL TO KEEP IT FROM SLIDING AROUND.

Chocolate Self-saucing Pudding

Serves 6

100 g butter, softened
¾ cups Chelsea White Sugar
1 egg
1 teaspoon vanilla essence
1¼ cups Champion standard grade flour
2 teaspoons Edmonds baking powder
1 tablespoon cocoa
½ cup Chelsea Soft Brown Sugar
1 tablespoon cornflour
¼ cup cocoa
2 cups boiling water

Preheat the oven to 180°C. Beat together the butter, sugar, egg and vanilla. In another bowl, sift the flour, baking powder and the first measure of cocoa together and fold into the beaten mixture. Spoon into a greased 6–8-cup ovenproof dish. Combine the brown sugar, cornflour and second measure of cocoa and carefully sprinkle this over the mixture in the dish (do not mix it in). Carefully pour the boiling water over the back of a spoon onto the pudding. Bake for 35 minutes or until the pudding springs back when lightly touched.

Christmas Pudding

SERVES 6–8

100 g butter
2 eggs
1 packed cup Chelsea Soft Brown Sugar
grated rind of 1 large lemon
grated rind of 1 orange
3 cups mixed fruit
1 large unpeeled apple finely chopped or grated
2 cups flour
1 teaspoon cinnamon
½ teaspoon ground cloves
1 teaspoon baking soda
juice of two oranges made up to 1 cup with brandy, rum or sherry

Melt the butter, then add the eggs and brown sugar and mix thoroughly. Add the lemon and orange rind, mixed fruit and apple and mix well. Sift in the flour, cinnamon, cloves and baking soda, and finally the cup of liquid. Mix until there are no pockets of flour. Pour into 1 large or 2 smaller buttered bowls that will fit inside large pots. The mixture should no more than three-quarters fill the bowl(s). Cover the bowl(s) with tinfoil. Lower each pudding bowl onto a saucer inside the larger pot. Add boiling water to the pot to come halfway up the bowl. Cover the pot tightly, bring back to the boil, then simmer gently for 4 hours, adding extra boiling water to the pot if the level falls.

If you are making this pudding ahead of time, refrigerate until required, then boil as before for another 2–3 hours before serving.

Serve with brandy butter or custard.

BRANDY BUTTER

125 g butter, softened
2 cups Chelsea Icing Sugar
1 tablespoon brandy

Beat or process all the ingredients together until light and creamy. Refrigerate until the butter hardens. Pile into a serving dish and serve at room temperature.

Citrus Tart

Serves 6

Base

125 g butter, softened
1 cup flour
½ cup Chelsea Icing Sugar

Filling

1 cup Chelsea Caster Sugar
½ cup lemon juice
grated rind of 2 lemons
2 tablespoons custard powder
½ teaspoon baking powder
3 eggs
Chelsea Icing Sugar to dust

First make the base. Place the butter, flour and icing sugar in a food processor and run the machine until the pastry clumps together in a ball around the blade. With floured hands press this mixture into the base and up the sides of a lined 21 cm loose-bottomed flan tin. Refrigerate for at least 30 minutes. (The pastry will set quite firm, but bakes best from cold.)

Preheat the oven to 180°C.

Place all the filling ingredients in the cleaned food processor and run the machine until well combined. Pour into the chilled base. Bake for 25 minutes until the pastry is crisp and golden and the filling set. Dust with icing sugar to serve.

Crème Caramel

Serves 6

¾ cup Chelsea White Sugar
½ cup water
2 cups milk
½ teaspoon vanilla essence
4 eggs
2 tablespoons Chelsea White Sugar

Preheat the oven to 180°C. Combine the first measure of sugar with the water in a heavy-bottomed saucepan. Gently heat, stirring constantly until the sugar has dissolved, then bring to the boil. Leave the syrup to boil *without stirring* until just golden, about 10 minutes. Working quickly, divide the syrup evenly between six individual ramekin dishes. Set aside.

Heat the milk until almost boiling, then remove it from the heat. Add the vanilla. In a separate bowl beat together the eggs and the second measure of sugar until pale. Pour the heated milk into this egg mixture and stir to combine. Strain.

Divide this mixture evenly between the caramel-lined dishes. Place the dishes in a roasting dish filled with enough water to come halfway up the sides of the ramekins. Bake for 35 minutes or until the custard is set. Remove the ramekins from the roasting dish and allow the custards to cool. Chill overnight, then tip from the moulds onto serving plates.

Golden Syrup Steamed Pudding

Serves 6

125 g butter, softened
½ cup Chelsea White Sugar
2 eggs
1 cup flour
2 teaspoons baking powder
½ teaspoon baking soda
¼ cup unsweetened yoghurt
½ cup Chelsea Golden Syrup

Cream the butter and sugar until light and fluffy. Add the eggs one at a time, beating well after each. Stir in the flour, baking powder and baking soda. Add the yoghurt and *half* the golden syrup and mix well. Lightly grease a pudding bowl, pour in the rest of the golden syrup and spoon the pudding mixture on top. Cover with lightly greased foil and secure with string. Place the bowl in a large saucepan half full of boiling water. Boil gently for 1½ hours, adding extra boiling water as it evaporates. Remove the bowl carefully and slide a knife around the pudding before turning it out. Serve warm with whipped cream.

A Chelsea Sugar recipe

Lemon Cheesecake

SERVES 8–10

Base
2 cups sweet biscuit crumbs
125 g butter, melted

Filling
1 packet lemon jelly crystals
¾ cup boiling water
¼ cup lemon juice
1 teaspoon grated lemon rind
375 g can evaporated milk, chilled
250 g cream cheese, softened
1 cup Chelsea Caster Sugar
1 teaspoon vanilla essence
whipped cream to decorate
fresh fruit to decorate

Preheat the oven to 180°C. Make the base by combining the biscuit crumbs and melted butter. Press onto the bottom and sides of a buttered 23 cm spring-form tin. Bake for 10 minutes. Cool and chill.

To make the filling, first dissolve the jelly crystals in the boiling water, add the lemon juice and rind and set aside to cool slightly. Meanwhile, beat the evaporated milk until thick. In another bowl beat the cream cheese until smooth and blend in the sugar, vanilla and beaten evaporated milk. Fold in the warm jelly mixture. Pour into the prepared base and chill for several hours or overnight. Decorate with whipped cream and fresh fruit.

Lemon Delicious Pudding

Serves 3–4

25 g butter, softened
1 cup Chelsea White Sugar
2 tablespoons self-raising flour
juice and grated rind of 2 medium lemons
1 cup milk
2 eggs, separated

Preheat the oven to 160°C. Cream the butter and sugar together until fluffy. Add the flour, lemon juice and rind, the milk and well-beaten egg yolks. Mix well. Beat the egg whites until stiff. Fold into the lemon mixture and pour into a well-greased pie dish of 4–6 cup capacity. Place the pie dish in a roasting pan and fill the pan with water to come three-quarters of the way up the sides of the pie dish. Bake for about 1 hour, until the pudding is set and lightly golden brown.

NOTE: This can be made in individual dishes, in which case allow a shorter cooking time: 30–40 minutes.

Lemon Meringue Pie

Serves 6–8

Pastry
2 tablespoons Chelsea White Sugar
1 egg
125 g butter, softened
1¾ cups flour
pinch salt
1 teaspoon baking powder

Filling
400 g can sweetened condensed milk
½ cup fresh lemon juice
1 tablespoon grated lemon rind
5 egg yolks

Meringue
5 egg whites
1½ cup Chelsea Caster Sugar

First make the pastry base. Beat the sugar and egg in a food processor until pale and frothy. In another bowl, mix together the butter, flour, salt and baking powder and add to the egg and sugar. Process until the mixture clumps together in a ball around the blade. Chill for 30 minutes, then press into the base and up the sides of a 23 cm loose-bottomed quiche or cake tin. Chill again for 30 minutes, then bake blind for 20–25 minutes at 180°C until golden and crisp.

Now to the filling. Mix all the ingredients together and pour into the cooked pastry shell.

For the meringue topping, beat the egg whites until stiff peaks form. Gradually beat in the caster sugar until it is all incorporated and the mixture is glossy. Pipe or pile over the lemon filling. Bake in a low oven (130–150°C) for 20–25 minutes until the meringue is firm and crisp. Cool in the tin. Remove when fully cold and serve with whipped cream or ice-cream. Cut with a wet knife and wipe the knife between cuts to neaten the slices.

Jo Seagar

Pavlova

Serves 8–10

6 egg whites, at room temperature
2 cups Chelsea Caster Sugar
1 teaspoon vanilla essence
1 teaspoon vinegar
2 teaspoons cornflour
300 ml cream, whipped
4–6 kiwifruit, peeled and sliced, for decoration
mint sprigs to garnish

Preheat the oven to 110°C. In a large metal, porcelain or glass (not plastic) bowl beat the egg whites until soft peaks form. Gradually, a teaspoonful at a time, add the caster sugar. The mixture should be getting glossy, thick and shiny with each addition and the whole sugar-adding process should take at least 10 minutes. Beat in the vanilla, vinegar and cornflour. Spoon the mixture out into a plate-sized mound on a baking-paper-covered tray. Bake for about 1½ hours until it is dry and crisp and lifts easily off the baking paper. Cool on a wire rack. To serve, place it flat side up on a serving plate, pile with whipped cream, cover with sliced kiwifruit and garnish with mint sprigs.

Rice Pudding

Serves 4

5 tablespoons short-grain rice
3 tablespoons Chelsea White Sugar
3 cups milk
½ teaspoon vanilla essence
1 teaspoon butter
freshly grated nutmeg (optional)

Preheat the oven to 150°C. Place the rice and sugar in a 4–6-cup ovenproof dish. Add the milk and vanilla and mix well. Add the knob of butter. Sprinkle a little nutmeg on top of the pudding and bake uncovered for about 2 hours, stirring several times during cooking. A golden brown skin will form on top as the pudding cooks. Stir this into the pudding every now and then, or remove it, depending on your taste. When the rice is very soft and the liquid is creamy, remove from the oven. Leave to stand for 15–30 minutes while it cools and thickens further.

Sticky Date Pudding with Butterscotch Sauce

Serves 6–8

1¼ cups pitted dates, chopped
1¼ cups boiling water
1 teaspoon baking soda
60 g butter, cubed
¾ cup Chelsea Soft Brown or Dark Cane Sugar
2 eggs
1 cup self-raising flour

Butterscotch Sauce

2 cups Chelsea Soft Brown or Dark Cane Sugar
1 cup (250 ml) cream
50 g butter
1 teaspoon vanilla essence

Combine all ingredients in medium-sized saucepan and stir over a low heat until the sugar has dissolved and the butter melted.

Preheat the oven to 180°C. Grease a deep 20 cm round cake tin and line the base with baking paper. Combine the dates, boiling water and soda in a bowl. Allow to stand for 5 minutes, then blend or process the date mixture with the butter and sugar until almost smooth. Add the eggs and flour, and blend or process until just combined. Pour into the prepared pan. Bake 45–50 minutes or until cooked through (cover the pudding with foil during baking if you think it's getting too brown on top). Stand the pudding for 10 minutes before turning it out of the pan. Pour butterscotch sauce over the top.

Jo's tip

IF YOUR BROWN SUGAR HAS GONE HARD IN STORAGE, TRY PUTTING IT IN THE MICROWAVE FOR A SHORT TIME.

A heritage recipe from New Zealand's cooking archives

Jams, Pickles & Sauces

Homemade jams, pickles and sauces are wonderful gifts for people you care about. They can really make a meal, by adding that little extra something to plain cold cuts, bread and cheese, or simple grilled chicken or fish. Jams and dessert sauces can also liven up ice-cream or a plain baked cake or muffin.

Turning excess produce into preserves to see you through the lean winter months is an ancient culinary art that has somehow gained an air of mystery in modern times. Yet the process is really very simple. It's just a matter of balancing the vegetable and fruit acids with sugar and pectin. We include here plenty of tips, hints and problem-solving ideas that will ensure your success every time.

Dried Apricot Jam	94
Lemon Curd	95
Microwave Mixed Berry Jam	96
Strawberry Jam	97
Three-fruit Marmalade	98
Pickled Onions	99
Tomato Relish	100
Barbecue Marinade	102
Caramel Sauce	103
Chocolate Sauce	104
Mint Sauce	105
Onion Marmalade Barbecue Sauce	106
Satay Sauce	108
Sweet & Sour Sauce	109

Left: Mint Sauce

Dried Apricot Jam

MAKES 6–7 CUPS

500 g dried apricots, chopped
6 cups water
1 tablespoon grated orange rind
½ cup fresh orange juice
2 tablespoons lemon juice
1 kg Chelsea White Sugar

Combine the apricots and water in a bowl, cover and stand overnight. Next day, combine the apricots and their liquid with the rind and orange and lemon juice in a large saucepan. Bring to the boil, then simmer for 20 minutes. Pour in the sugar and stir until it dissolves, then bring the mixture back to the boil. Without stirring too often, boil gently for about an hour until the jam gels when tested. Pour into hot sterilised jars and seal when cold.

A Chelsea Sugar recipe

Lemon Curd

Makes 2½–3 cups

rind and juice of 4 lemons
125 g butter, melted
2 cups Chelsea Caster Sugar
4 eggs, beaten

Mix all ingredients in the top of a double-boiler and stir over boiling water until the mixture thickens. Pour into sterilised jars and store in the refrigerator.

Jo's tip

When juicing citrus, microwave the whole fruit on high for 15–20 seconds and it will squeeze more easily.

A Chelsea Sugar recipe

Microwave Mixed Berry Jam

MAKES 2½ CUPS

500 g berries (raspberries, blackberries, etc)
2 cups Chelsea White Sugar
1 teaspoon lemon juice

Place the berries in a deep microwave-safe bowl and cook on high power for 2 minutes. Stir in the sugar and lemon juice, cook on high for 5 minutes, then stir. Cook for a further 5–8 minutes until the jam setting point is reached (104°C). (A jam or sugar thermometer eliminates all the guesswork.) Pour into warm sterilised jars and seal.

Jo's tip

TO STERILISE JARS IN THE MICROWAVE, HALF FILL THEM WITH COLD WATER AND COOK ON HIGH FOR 2–3 MINUTES UNTIL THE WATER BOILS. CAREFULLY TIP OUT THE WATER AND FILL THE JARS WITH JAM WHILE STILL WARM.

Strawberry Jam

MAKES ABOUT 4 CUPS

1 kg strawberries, hulled
6 cups Chelsea White Sugar
1½ teaspoons tartaric acid

Put the strawberries into a preserving pan. Crush them lightly with a potato masher or fork. Add the sugar and stir thoroughly. Bring to the boil and boil for 5 minutes. Add the tartaric acid and boil rapidly for a further 5 minutes. Pour into sterilised jars.

Jo's tip

FRESH, FROZEN OR CANNED FRUITS ARE GENERALLY INTERCHANGEABLE IN EQUAL MEASURES IN RECIPES.

A Chelsea Sugar recipe

Three-fruit Marmalade

MAKES 7–8 CUPS

4 large oranges
2 lemons
1 grapefruit
5 cups water
6 cups (approx.) Chelsea White Sugar

Wash the fruit and cut in half. With a sharp knife, cut the halves into thin slices. Remove the pips and tie them into a piece of muslin. Place the fruit, any juice that has escaped, the muslin bag of pips and the water in a large bowl. Cover and let stand overnight.

The next day transfer the mixture to a large pot. Bring to the boil and simmer, covered, for 1 hour or until the rind is soft. Discard the muslin bag. Measure the fruit mixture and return it to the saucepan with ¾ cup sugar to each cup of fruit mixture. Stir over a gentle heat to dissolve the sugar, then bring to the boil. Boil uncovered (don't stir too often) for 40 minutes or until the marmalade gels when tested. Pour into hot sterilised jars and seal when cold.

Pickled Onions

Makes 3 jars

1 kg small pickling onions, peeled and left whole
½ cup salt
5 cups water
1 litre malt vinegar
½ cup Chelsea White Sugar
1 tablespoon pickling spice

Put the onions, salt and water in a large bowl. Cover and stand overnight. Next day, drain the onions and rinse well under cold running water. Pack them into 500 ml sterilised jars. Combine the remaining ingredients in a large saucepan. Stir over a medium heat as you bring the mixture to the boil. Then turn down the heat and simmer for 10 minutes. Cool. Strain the cold vinegar mixture over the onions to cover completely, and seal the jars.

Jo's tip

You can customise pickled onions by adding sprigs of herbs, chillies, garlic, cloves or different spices to subtlely change the flavour.

A Chelsea Sugar recipe

Tomato Relish

Makes 6 cups

1.5 kg tomatoes, blanched, skinned and quartered
4 onions, peeled and quartered
2 tablespoons salt
2 cups Chelsea Soft Brown Sugar
2¼ cups vinegar
3 chillies, deseeded and finely chopped
1 tablespoon mustard powder
1 tablespoon curry powder
2 tablespoons Champion standard grade flour
¼ cup vinegar

Put the tomatoes and onions into a non-metal bowl. Sprinkle with salt and leave for 12 hours, then drain off the liquid that has formed. Put the vegetables, sugar, first measure of vinegar and chillies into a preserving pan. Boil gently for 1½ hours, stirring frequently. Mix the mustard, curry powder, flour and second measure of vinegar to a smooth paste. Stir into the relish and boil for 5 minutes. Pack into hot, dry jars and seal.

Jo's tip

END OF SEASON, GREEN OR UNDER-RIPE TOMATOES ARE IDEAL FOR TOMATO RELISH.

Barbecue Marinade

Makes 1 cup

2 tablespoons soy sauce
2 tablespoons Chelsea Dark Cane Sugar
¼ cup vinegar
1 teaspoon crushed garlic (1–2 cloves)
1 teaspoon grated fresh ginger
1 tablespoon smooth Dijon-style mustard
1 tablespoon cornflour mixed with
  ½ cup cold water

Mix all ingredients in a blender or whisk well in a bowl. Place in a small saucepan and bring to the boil, stirring continuously. Remove from the heat and cool. Store in the refrigerator. Marinate meat for 2–3 hours for maximum flavour and tenderising.

Caramel Sauce

MAKES 3 CUPS

2 cups Chelsea Soft Brown Sugar
300 ml cream
50 g butter
1 teaspoon vanilla essence

Combine all ingredients in a medium-sized saucepan. Stir over a low heat until the sugar has dissolved and butter melted. Store any unused sauce in the refrigerator for up to 10 days.

Jo Seagar

Chocolate Sauce

Makes 1½ cups

2 tablespoons cornflour
¼ cup cocoa
a little cold water
1 cup hot water
¼ cup Chelsea Caster Sugar
25 g butter
1 teaspoon vanilla essence

In a medium-sized saucepan blend the cornflour and cocoa with a little cold water to make a smooth paste. Stir in the hot water, caster sugar and butter. Stir over a gentle heat until the mixture comes to the boil and thickens. Add the vanilla. Cool and store in the refrigerator. Serve over ice-cream or steamed puddings. (The sauce may need to be warmed if it sets too hard in the refrigerator.)

Jo's tip

Another very simple rich chocolate sauce recipe is 1 cup of cream and 200 g chocolate melted together over gentle heat, stirring until well combined. This must be served warm as it sets solid at room temperature.

A Chelsea Sugar recipe

Mint Sauce

Makes about 1 cup

¼ cup finely chopped fresh mint leaves
boiling water
2 tablespoons Chelsea White Sugar
½ cup vinegar
salt

Place the chopped mint in a jug and just cover with boiling water. Add the sugar and vinegar, then salt to taste. No roast lamb would be complete without it!

Jo's tip

Excess crops of herbs can be stored in small bags in the freezer; or for herbs like mint and basil, chop the leaves finely and freeze in icecube trays. Each cube is approx. 1 teaspoon of chopped herb.

A heritage recipe from New Zealand's cooking archives

Onion Marmalade Barbecue Sauce

MAKES 2–3 CUPS

6 medium onions, finely chopped
¼ cup Chelsea Raw Sugar
1½ cups beef stock
¼ cup balsamic or red wine vinegar
4 tablespoons grainy whole-seed mustard
250 g sour cream or light sour cream
3 tablespoons chopped parsley

Place the chopped onion in a large frying pan with the raw sugar and beef stock. Simmer over a moderate heat for 45–50 minutes until the liquid has evaporated and the onions are caramelised and golden brown. Stir in the vinegar and mustard.

This is your basic onion marmalade, which can be used as a topping for crostini or served on toast fingers with paté. It keeps well in the fridge.

It can also be made into a special barbecue sauce. Gently warm the onion marmalade and add the sour cream and chopped parsley. Serve warm or at room temperature as a great sauce for barbecued meats, or cold as a dip.

A Chelsea Sugar recipe

Satay Sauce

MAKES 2½ CUPS

¼ cup oil
1 teaspoon crushed garlic (2–3 cloves)
1 large onion, finely chopped
1 teaspoon chilli powder (or to taste)
1 cup crunchy peanut butter
2 tablespoons soy sauce
2 tablespoons lemon juice
½ cup Chelsea Dark Cane Sugar
1½ cups coconut cream
salt and pepper to taste

Heat the oil in a saucepan. Add the garlic, onion and chilli powder and cook for 2 minutes over a medium heat. Stir in the peanut butter, soy sauce, lemon juice and sugar. Add the coconut cream, bring to the boil and season with salt and pepper to taste. Serve over beef or chicken satays, barbecued meat or with burgers.

Jo's tip

DISPOSABLE WATER BOTTLES MAKE GREAT DISPENSERS FOR SALAD DRESSINGS, OILS AND SAUCES.

A Chelsea Sugar recipe

Sweet & Sour Sauce

Makes 2 cups

225 g can pineapple pieces in juice
1 tablespoon Chelsea Soft Brown or Dark Cane Sugar
½ cup vinegar
1 tablespoon soy sauce
2 tablespoons tomato paste
1 tablespoon sweet chilli sauce
2 spring onions, finely sliced
½ small deseeded red pepper, finely chopped or sliced
2 tablespoons cornflour
1 cup water

Combine all ingredients except the cornflour and water in a medium saucepan. Bring to the boil. Blend the cornflour and water together and stir into the mixture. Simmer for 4–5 minutes to thicken.

Jo's tip

THIS SAUCE IS WONDERFUL ADDED TO STIR-FRIED VEGETABLES, AS PHOTOGRAPHED.

A Chelsea Sugar recipe

Index

Afghans   8
Anzac Biscuits   9
Apple Cinnamon Cake   36
Apple Crumble   74
Apricot Balls   64
Apricot Crunch Muffins   54
Apricot Jam, Dried   94

Baby Pecan Pies   10
Banana Bran Muffins   55
Banana Cake, Moist   47
Barbecue Marinade   102
Biscuits
    Afghans   8
    Anzac Biscuits   9
    Baby Pecan Pies   10
    Chelsea Muesli Bars   12
    Chocolate Chip Biscuits   13
    Chocolate Chunk Oat Cookies   14
    Coconut Macaroons   18
    Ginger Snaps   22
    Hokey Pokey Biscuits   23
    Melting Moments   25
    Meringues   26
    Peanut Brownie Biscuits   28
    Pikelets   29
    Shortbread   30
    Sugar-crusted Vanilla Cupcakes   31
    see also Slices
Blueberry Muffins   56
Brandy Butter   78
Bread & Butter Pudding   75
Brownies
    Double Chocolate Fudge Brownies   19
    Peanut Brownie Biscuits   28
Butterscotch Sauce   90

Cakes
    Apple Cinnamon Cake   36
    Carrot Cake   37
    Celebration Chocolate Cake   38
    Classic Chocolate Cake   39
    Date & Walnut Loaf   40
    Gingerbread   42
    Lemon Syrup Loaf   43
    Marble Cake   45
    Mississippi Mud Cake   46
    Moist Banana Cake   47
    Rich Christmas Cake   48
    Sponge Cake   49
    Sultana Cake   50
Caramel Sauce   103
Caramel Slice   11
Carrot Cake   37
Celebration Chocolate Cake   38
Cheesecake, Lemon   84
Chelsea Muesli Bars   12
Chocolate
    Celebration Chocolate Cake   38
    Classic Chocolate Cake   39
    Double Chocolate Fudge Brownies   19
    Jaffa Muffins   60
    Mississippi Mud Cake   46
    White Chocolate Chunk Muffins   61
    & see below
Chocolate Chip Biscuits   13
Chocolate Chip Muffins   57
Chocolate Chunk Oat Cookies   14
Chocolate Fudge Square   15
Chocolate Fudge   65
Chocolate Icing   11
Chocolate Mousse   76
Chocolate Peppermint Slice   16
Chocolate Prune & Port Truffles   66
Chocolate Rum & Raisin Balls   68
Chocolate Sauce   104
Chocolate Self-saucing Pudding   77
Christmas Cake, Rich   48

Christmas Pudding   78
Citrus Tart   81
Classic Chocolate Cake   39
Coconut Ice   69
Coconut Macaroons   18
Cookies *see* Biscuits
Custard Squares, Vanilla   32
Cream Cheese Frosting   37
Crème Caramel   82
Crunchy Lemon Poppyseed Muffins   58
Cupcakes, Sugar-crusted Vanilla   31

Date & Walnut Loaf   40
Desserts
    Apple Crumble   74
    Bread & Butter Pudding   75
    Chocolate Mousse   76
    Chocolate Self-saucing Pudding   77
    Christmas Pudding   78
    Citrus Tart   81
    Crème Caramel   82
    Golden Syrup Steamed Pudding   83
    Lemon Cheesecake   84
    Lemon Delicious Pudding   86
    Lemon Meringue Pie   87
    Pavlova   88
    Rice Pudding   89
    Sticky Date Pudding with Butterscotch Sauce   90
Double Chocolate Fudge Brownies   19
Dried Apricot Jam   94

Fudge
    Chocolate Fudge Square   15
    Chocolate Fudge   65
    Russian Fudge   71

Ginger Crunch   20
Ginger Icing   20
Ginger Snaps   22
Gingerbread   42
Golden Syrup Steamed Pudding   83

Hokey Pokey Biscuits   23
Hokey Pokey   70

Icing
    Chocolate Icing   11
    Cream Cheese Frosting   37
    Ginger Icing   20
    Lemon Icing   47
    Vanilla Icing   32

Jaffa Muffins   60
Jam
    Dried Apricot Jam   94
    Lemon Curd   95
    Microwave Mixed Berry Jam   96
    Strawberry Jam   97
    Three-fruit Marmalade   98

Lemon
    Citrus Tart   81
    Crunchy Lemon Poppyseed Muffins   58
    & see below
Lemon Cheesecake   84
Lemon Curd   95
Lemon Delicious Pudding   86
Lemon Icing   47
Lemon Meringue Pie   87
Lemon Syrup Loaf   43
Loaf
    Date & Walnut Loaf   40
    Gingerbread   42
    Lemon Syrup Loaf   43
Louise Cake   24

Macaroons, Coconut   18
Marble Cake   45
Marinade, Barbecue   102
Marmalade
    Onion Marmalade Barbecue Sauce   106
    Three-fruit Marmalade   98
Melting Moments   25
Meringues   26; *see also* Lemon Meringue Pie   87, Pavlova   88

Microwave Mixed Berry Jam   96
Mint Sauce   105
Mississippi Mud Cake   46
Moist Banana Cake   47
Mousse, Chocolate   76
Muesli Bars, Chelsea   12
Muffins
    Apricot Crunch Muffins   54
    Banana Bran Muffins   55
    Blueberry Muffins   56
    Chocolate Chip Muffins   57
    Crunchy Lemon Poppyseed Muffins   58
    Jaffa Muffins   60
    White Chocolate Chunk Muffins   61

Onion Marmalade Barbecue Sauce   106
Onions, Pickled   99

Pavlova   88
Peanut Brownie Biscuits   28
Pecan Pies, Baby   10
Pickled Onions   99
Pickles
    Pickled Onions   99
    Tomato Relish   100
Pies
    Baby Pecan Pies   10
    Citrus Tart   81
    Lemon Meringue Pie   87
Pikelets   29
Puddings: *see* Desserts

Relish, Tomato   100
Rice Pudding   89
Rich Christmas Cake   48
Russian Fudge   71

Satay Sauce   108
Sauces
    Barbecue Marinade   102
    Brandy Butter   78
    Butterscotch Sauce   90

Caramel Sauce   103
Chocolate Sauce   104
Mint Sauce   105
Onion Marmalade Barbecue Sauce   106
Satay Sauce   108
Sweet & Sour Sauce   109
Shortbread   30
Slices
    Caramel Slice   11
    Chocolate Fudge Square   15
    Chocolate Peppermint Slice   16
    Double Chocolate Fudge Brownies   19
    Ginger Crunch   20
    Louise Cake   24
    Vanilla Custard Squares   32
Sponge Cake   49
Steamed Pudding, Golden Syrup   83
Sticky Date Pudding with Butterscotch
    Sauce   90
Strawberry Jam   97
Sugar-crusted Vanilla Cupcakes   31
Sultana Cake   50
Sweet & Sour Sauce   109
Sweets
    Apricot Balls   64
    Chocolate Fudge   65
    Chocolate Prune & Port Truffles   66
    Chocolate Rum & Raisin Balls   68
    Coconut Ice   69
    Hokey Pokey   70
    Russian Fudge   71

Three-fruit Marmalade   98
Tomato Relish   100
Truffles
    Chocolate Prune & Port Truffles   66
    Chocolate Rum & Raisin Balls   68

Vanilla Custard Squares   32
Vanilla Icing   32

White Chocolate Chunk Muffins   61